THE EAST COAST MAIN LINE
KING'S CROSS TO PETERBOROUGH

Adam Head

AMBERLEY

First published 2019

Amberley Publishing
The Hill, Stroud
Gloucestershire, GL5 4EP

www.amberley-books.com

Copyright © Adam Head, 2019

The right of Adam Head to be identified as
the Author of this work has been asserted in
accordance with the Copyrights, Designs and
Patents Act 1988.

ISBN 978 1 4456 8746 9 (print)
ISBN 978 1 4456 8747 6 (ebook)

British Library Cataloguing in Publication Data.
A catalogue record for this book is available from
the British Library.

Origination by Amberley Publishing.
Printed in the UK.

Contents

Introduction

One of Britain's most exquisite main lines, the East Coast Main Line opened fully in 1850. The line runs a total of 393 miles from England's bustling London to Scotland's lively Edinburgh, stopping at places along the way, all with their own unique charm.

This book covers the first 76 miles from London King's Cross to its first major stop on the East Coast Main Line at Peterborough in Cambridgeshire. While travelling from London to Peterborough a traveller will pass through twenty-four stations and four different counties, with the average time between these two stations being roughly one hour. The stations between London King's Cross and Peterborough are as follows:

- London King's Cross
- Finsbury Park*
- Harringay
- Hornsey
- Alexandra Palace
- New Southgate
- Oakleigh Park
- New Barnet
- Hadley Wood
- Potters Bar
- Brookmans Park
- Welham Green
- Hatfield
- Welwyn Garden City
- Welwyn North
- Knebworth
- Stevenage
- Hitchin
- Arlesey
- Biggleswade
- Sandy
- St Neots
- Huntingdon
- Peterborough

* At Finsbury Park the Northern City line turns off to the left and continues for another 3 miles to Moorgate, stopping at six stations along the way. The Class 313 EMU is the only unit that is allowed to operate this line due to the dual voltage system in place and the width of the tunnels after Drayton Park. It is from this station that the 313s stop using 25 kV AC from the overhead lines and start using 750 V DC from the third rail underneath the 313 using a third rail shoe. Many of the stations on this line are still decorated in Network SouthEast colours and signs, despite it being disbanded in 1994.

Between London King's Cross and Peterborough there is also a 24-mile loop from Stevenage to Alexandra Palace known as the Hertford loop line. This can act as a diversionary route should there be any engineering works or issues on the East Coast Main Line. Just like the rest of the East Coast Main Line, this loop is electrified and has an hourly service from Stevenage and Watton-on-Stone to Moorgate, stopping at all stations on the Hertford loop.

Current ECML Operators

All journeys to Scotland and the north start from the beautiful London King's Cross station, which was built in 1852 by Lewis Cubitt and remained mainly unchanged until refurbishment started in 2007. A new concourse opened in 2012, followed by the original entrance opening in 2013.

There are four train operating companies that provide services out of London King's Cross, but only two stop at Peterborough.

The first operator, London North Eastern Railway, is the largest operator on the East Coast Main Line, and its bright and vibrant colours aren't difficult to miss. They operate fast services from London King's Cross to places such as Leeds, York, Edinburgh and Inverness. With all their routes, stock on the LNER travels a total of 936 miles. Their stock comprises thirty-two HST power cars with British Rail Mk 3 carriages and thirty-one Class 91s with British Rail Mk 4 carriages, as well as Class 82 driving van trailers (DVTs).

Left: The Virgin East Coast Trains logo, as seen on the iconic HST.

Right: The London North Eastern Railway (LNER) logo, also seen on the iconic HST.

At the time of writing, London North Eastern Railway is currently in the process of acquiring sixty-five brand-new Class 800s, which are known as Azumas (Japanese for 'east'). These Azumas will replace all of the LNER's current stock from the end of 2018.

London North Eastern Railway started operating on 24 July 2018 after the previous operator, Virgin East Coast Trains, which started running the ECML in 2015, gave up its franchise after running into financial difficulties and had to return it. From 2009, LNER, much like East Coast, became a nationalised operator on the East Coast Main Line.

The second operator is the other main operator of the East Coast Main Line known as Great Northern/Thameslink (part of Govia Thameslink Railway), which runs a mixture of fast, semi-fast and slow services to destinations such as Peterborough, Cambridge, Ely and King's Lynn. Great Northern also runs services to Moorgate from Letchworth Garden City and Welwyn Garden City. Its stock differs greatly to Virgin East Coast Trains, as its only consists of electric multiple units. Its units vary between a mix of the old and the new as it operates forty[*] Class 365 Networker EMUs and twenty-nine Class 387 Electrostar EMUs. However, Thameslink is now introducing newer Class 700 Desiro EMUs that are starting to make appearances on the East Coast Main Line, replacing the older Class 365 Networker EMUs.

There are two open access operators that also provide services on the East Coast Main Line. The first is Grand Central, which has been operating since 2007, providing a unique service between London and Sunderland via York and Hartlepool before starting another unique service in 2010 to Bradford via Doncaster and Halifax. In 2011 Grand Central was acquired by the Arriva Group and continues to operate under the same name. When Grand Central first started operating it ran a small fleet of HSTs with six power cars, but its fleet was later boosted with the arrival of five Class 180 Adelante DMUs, which allowed it to run more frequent services. In 2017, after ten years of operating, Grand Central retired its HSTs in favour of running a complete fleet of Class 180 Adelantes, receiving more units from First Great Western. After running a farewell tour for its HSTs, they were later transferred to East Midlands Trains.

---

[*]At the time of writing some of the Class 365 Networkers were starting to be transferred to Scotland to work Edinburgh Waverley–Glasgow Queen Street services, or else they were going into storage.

Above left: The Great Northern logo, as seen on one of its former Class 317 EMUs.

Above right: The Grand Central logo, as seen on one of its former HSTs.

Right: The First Hull Trains logo, as seen on a Class 180 Adelante.

The second open access operator on the East Coast Main Line is First Hull Trains (originally Hull Trains) and it has been operating since 2000, providing a fast service from London King's Cross to Hull via Selby. In 2008 it then became part of the First Group and became First Hull Trains. At the time of writing its trains comprise four Class 180 Adelantes, which were repainted into First's very attractive and eye-catching corporate colours. Its stock, however, unlike the other East Coast Main Line operators, has changed several times. When its services first started running it was borrowing Class 170 Turbostars from Anglia Railways, until its own Class 170 Turbostars arrived in 2004. However, the Class 170 Turbostars were replaced in 2005 with faster and larger Class 222 Pioneers, which had four carriages and a maximum speed of 125 mph, compared to the Class 170 Turbostars' three carriages and 100 mph maximum speed. This became the normal routine on the East Coast Main Line until 2007, when one of the Pioneers (No. 222103) became severely damaged when it fell off the jacks while undergoing routine maintenance. Because of this accident Hull Trains was short a unit, so in 2008 it hired an unusual choice of train in the form of No. 86101, which used British Rail Mk 3 carriages and a Class 82 driving van trailer (No. 82115) to work shuttle services from London King's Cross to Doncaster. Finally, in 2008 four Class 180 Adelantes were brought in to replace all four of the Class 222 Pioneers, which transferred to East Midlands Trains and joined its fleet of twenty-three Class 222 Meridians.

Previous Operators

Many operators ran on the East Coast Main Line after privatisation arrived in the late 1990s, all with their various colour schemes.

When privatisation arrived, the first operator to take over from Intercity (after sectorisation of British Railways in the 1980s) was Great Northern Eastern Railway, which wasted no time in unleashing its new colour scheme of blue and red on the East Coast Main Line and making it its own. GNER inherited the fleet of Class 43 HSTs and Class 91s from Intercity and throughout the duration of its franchise upgraded them and refurbished them. The HSTs received new engines, with their old Paxman Valentas being replaced with MTU engines, while the Mk 3s underwent a thorough refurbishment. The same applied for the Class 91s in the 2000s, with the locos receiving a complete refurbishments, resulting in their reliability going up. Moreover, the Mk 4 carriages received a complete refresh under the project name Mallard, after the famous A4 Pacific locomotive, which holds the world record for fastest steam locomotive in the world at 126 mph.

Sadly in 2007 GNER's parent company had to give up the East Coast Main Line franchise after it encountered financial difficulties. As a result, the franchise was put up for tender again.

In 2007 the East Coast Main Line franchise was awarded to National Express, which aptly named it National Express East Coast (its franchise naming was dubious after naming its East Anglian franchise ONE). Just like GNER it didn't waste any time in making its presence known, with the familiar red stripe on the GNER's old trains being changed to a white stripe. It carried on where GNER had left off with the upgrade of the HSTs, with them receiving the National Express house colours of silver and white. While the HSTs received a lot of attention, the Class 91s did not, as only one made it into National Express colours (No. 91111). The rest of the fleet never made it into a new livery, wearing GNER dark blue with a white interim stripe across the middle.

In 2009 it was discovered that National Express had paid too much for the East Coast franchise and that due to external situations, such as a downward economy, the company was struggling to make ends meet. In the end the government decided not to help National Express and as a result it had to hand back the franchise. However, instead of it being put up for tender again, something unexpected happened.

In November 2009, and for the first time since 1996, the East Coast Main Line had gone back into public ownership, with the new, and again aptly named, East Coast taking over operations. East Coast was a subsidiary of Directly Operated Railways for the Department for Transport and this meant another livery change, with all the HSTs sets and the Class 91s receiving a new livery of grey and purple.

Much like with GNER and National Express, with East Coast there was no new stock introduced, instead making good use of what it already had. One change was made regarding the Class 91s, however, with them starting to be renamed after they had been de-named during the National Express era. As an example, No. 91109 was named *Sir Bobby Robson* in 2011, with Nos 91110 and 91107 being named in 2012 and 2013 respectively. The last loco under East Coast's management was No. 91111, which was named and also unveiled in a new livery in 2014 for the 100th anniversary of the beginning of the First World War.

There have been changes to the other main operator of the East Coast Main Line after Network Southeast was to be no more. After privatisation the first franchise owner for London to Cambridge and Peterborough services was WAGN (West Anglia Great Northern), which inherited a wide range of electric multiple units from Network SouthEast, which included forty-one Class 313s, eighteen Class 315s, seventy-two Class 317s and forty Class 365 Networkers. All but the Class 365 Networkers received the new purple livery of WAGN. WAGN operated services between Cambridge and London Liverpool Street, as well as London King's Cross until 2004, when it was announced that there would be a strategic reorganisation of franchises. As a result, the services from Cambridge to London Liverpool Street became part of the new Greater Anglia franchise. Unfortunately for WAGN, the new franchise was given to National Express.

Another strategic reorganisation of franchises spelled bad luck for WAGN as it was announced that the Great Northern services were to be merged with the Thameslink services. When the new franchise was announced, it was declared it had been awarded to First.

In April 2006, a new franchise emerged on the East Coast Main Line in the form of First Capital Connect, which would start running the services from London to Peterborough, King's Lynn and Cambridge. It wasn't too long before it would start putting its eye-catching livery of neon blue and purple on to its trains, which were all inherited from the Great Northern side of WAGN.

In 2010 First Capital Connect increased its EMU fleet with thirteen Class 321/4s. These were no longer required by London Midland and were pushed onto the East Coast Main Line in the hope of easing the overcrowding that plagued the East Coast Main Line, allowing eight-carriage trains to become twelve-carriage trains during peak times.

In 2012 it was announced that a new franchise was going to be created, which would merge the Great Northern, Thameslink and Southern areas all together to make one operator for the entire area. Unfortunately, it didn't fall in First's favour, with the company losing out to rivals Govia. As a result First Capital Connect ran on the East Coast Main Line until 2014, when Great Northern, the current incumbent, started operations on 14 September.

The Trains of the ECML

The East Coast Main Line is synonymous with pioneering trains, beginning with the A4s with their streamlined looks and their record-beating capabilities. Or rather, this was the case until the early 1960s, when steam was being replaced with diesel throughout the railway network. Thus, the successors to these very successful locomotives were the Class 55 Deltics, which were built between 1961 and 1962 at Newton-le Willows. These unique locomotives were allocated to three depots on the East Coast Main Line: Finsbury Park in East London, Gateshead in Newcastle and Haymarket in Scotland.

These locos were unique due to the engine that was fitted in them, with no other diesel locomotive ever having this type of engine. The engine was designed in a triangle shape and had three cylinders. There were two of these engines in each loco, each producing 1,650 hp each. So with a total of 3,300 hp, the Class 55 Deltic was the most powerful diesel locomotive on the British Rail network at the time, with 100 mph being obtainable.

The Deltics took over the A4s' work and were being delivered in BR two-tone green before the entire fleet became BR corporate blue. Moreover, with the extra power that they were bringing to the East Coast Main Line, it meant that the timetable could be overhauled, and as a result services between London King's Cross and Edinburgh took less time. The Deltics ruled the East Coast Main Line until the late 1970s, when the iconic HST was designed and built. As a result the Deltics were taken off the main express services to be put onto lower priority semi-fast services from London King's Cross.

As more and more HSTs arrived onto the East Coast Main Line, with thirty-two sets being allocated to the Eastern Region, a new timetable was brought into effect in 1979. When a full HST start came, the Deltics were starting to be withdrawn. This was because maintenance was becoming more and more necessary and they couldn't be transferred to other areas of the British Railways network due to a lack of crew knowledge. The first Deltic was withdrawn in 1980, with the last one being withdrawn in December 1981. The Deltics didn't leave the East Coast Main Line unnoticed though, as a railtour from London King's Cross to Edinburgh was laid on, and this was very popular with train enthusiasts.

The transition from Deltics to HSTs on the East Coast Main Line was painless and on 8 May 1978 a regular 125 mph service was launched between London King's Cross, Newcastle and Edinburgh. Becoming a staple of East Coast Main Line life, more HSTs were introduced and more locations, such as Leeds and Aberdeen, were soon added. Then, as passengers were introduced to increased comfort and faster train services, it didn't take long for passenger numbers to begin to increase.

It wasn't only the passengers that would take a liking to the HSTs as train enthusiasts loved the screaming 2,250 hp Paxman Valenta 12RP200L engine, which could be heard for some distance away and would make a noticeable sight when power was applied, emitting large amount of exhaust fumes (or clag to enthusiasts), which only cemented their high reputation as one of British Railways' most successful high-speed passenger trains.

The HSTs would continue to dominate the East Coast Main Line until it was announced in 1984 that the East Coast Main Line was to be electrified, meaning that new electric trains would need to be built.

In 1988 the first Class 91 electric locomotive rolled off the production line in Crewe. Built by GEC (General Electric Company), which was a sub-contractor of BREL (British Rail Engineering Limited), another thirty Class 91s followed between 1988 and 1991 to replace the HSTs as the main train of the East Coast Main Line. With a faster acceleration and a higher top speed, the concept of a loco hauling carriages was kept over the possibility of using a unit formation instead.

As electrification reached further and further up the East Coast Main Line, the Class 91s were sure to follow. The first Class 91 built, No. 91001, reached Leeds on 11 August 1988. Six months later the Class 91s were drafted into public service, with the first diagram operated, the 17.36 London King's Cross–Peterborough service, being worked by No. 91001. The locos started to work to Leeds eight days later, with No. 91008 working the 06.50 London King's Cross–Leeds service.

The Class 91s were built and delivered promptly, but the rest of the train was not yet ready. Because of the issue with the Class 82 DVTs not being ready, they fell back on the trusty HST to help, with power cars being made into driving van trailers. They had buffers fixed to the front of the loco and new equipment installed, such as a TDM (Time Division Multiplexer). Once newer Mk 4 carriages had been introduced into service, these HST surrogate DVTs could go back to their old duties.

But after more than thirty years in use delivering passengers up and the down the East Coast Main Line, the future is set to change, with new trains being built by Hitachi that are due to replace both the HSTs and the Class 91s. The Class 800/801 Intercity Express Train (IET), built in Newton Aycliffe, will come in two subclasses: the 800/1 and 800/2; and the 801/1 and 801/2. Both the 800s and 801s will be built to nine and five-carriage formations, with their only main difference being that the 800 is a bi-mode unit, allowing it to continue operating under diesel power should the OHLE be unavailable for any reason.

These new futuristic trains have already started to be tested on the East Coast Main Line in hopes that they will start operating at the end of 2018.

The Nene Valley Railway

At the end of this section of the East Coast Main Line is the Nene Valley Railway at Wansford, where an entirely volunteer-based group of people work hard to keep a 7.5-mile single-track preserved line running to Peterborough via Orton Mere.

This line used to be part of the Northampton–Peterborough line, which ran from Blisworth via Northampton Bridge Street towards Peterborough East, allowing connections for passengers travelling towards Norwich, Cambridge and other places in East Anglia. At one point Wansford was a very important junction as passengers would be able to reach places such as Leicester, Northampton and Rugby as it was served by the Great Northern Railway and the London North Western Railway. The station has a waiting room known as 'The Barnwell Building'. This was used by members of the Royal Family when they visited Barnwell Manor, which was the home of HRH the Duke of Gloucester. The building was moved from Barnwell station in 1977, thirteen years after it closed in 1964, and now sits on Platform 2, fully restored to its former glory.

This line was also a victim of the Beeching Axe as fewer and fewer passengers used this line in favour of the car. Therefore, the withdrawal of passenger services between Northampton Bridge Street and Peterborough North occurred in July 1963, and despite many lines being closed around the country, this was met with opposition. Unfortunately this wasn't enough and the line was closed to passenger services in May 1964, although iron ore freight trains continued to run until 1966. British Railways withdrew all freight by 1972.

However, in 1974 a group known as the Peterborough Development Corporation bought a section of the line between Longville and Yarwell Junction and leased it to a group known as the Peterborough Railway Society, which had formed in 1968. Three years later, in June 1977, the Nene Valley Railway was born and services started to run between Wansford and Orton Mere, with the railway receiving locos from other areas of the UK, as well as Denmark and France.

Despite a few issues, such as lack of facilities at Wansford and the station of Orton Mere being unfindable to people who weren't familiar with the area, the Nene Valley Railway continued to prosper. A turntable was installed at Wansford in 1978, along with a new engine shed five years later, as well as an extension of the line to Yarwell Junction. A year later, in 1984, the Nene Valley Railway started an appeal to extend the line out to Peterborough. This took place in 1986, but the railway was unable to use the original Peterborough East station, which had been closed in 1970 and subsequently demolished two years later, with only one of the platforms still standing to this day. Therefore a new station needed to be built, which was named Peterborough

Nene Valley. The station has views of both the East Coast Main Line and the Ely–Peterborough line from both the platform and the station car park.

Also based at Peterborough Nene Valley is Railworld, which can't be missed as it houses the remains of RTV31, a tracked hovercraft that was part of an experiment that unfortunately never came to fruition. Railworld also offers many other exhibits and a large OO gauge model railway featuring everyone's favourite steam engine, Thomas the Tank Engine, and his friends.

The Nene Valley Railway is also famous for being a regular place for filming, having been used on two occasions to film James Bond. In 1982 Wansford station was used to film parts of *Octopussy*, and in 1995 the line was used again to film parts of *Goldeneye* using a heavily disguised Class 20 diesel locomotive. Bands such as Queen used the Nene Valley Railway to create the music video for the song 'Breakthru', the video consisted of the band performing on an open platform behind a moving train on the line. Television shows such as *Casualty, EastEnders, London's Burning* and *The South Bank Show* have all filmed here too.

Every year the Nene Valley is open near enough all year round and has a variety of different events using both steam and diesel locomotives. There is something for everyone at the Nene Valley Railway, which can be accessed by road from either end of the railway or is a short walk away from Peterborough station itself.

A short walk away from Peterborough station is the Nene Valley Railway. At 7.5 miles long, this railway operates both steam and diesel locomotives and has many events, with there being at least one diesel gala held every year. In 2016 an East Coast Main Line favourite came in the form of Class 55 Deltic No. 55022, which at this event was disguised as No. 55007 *Pinza*. Here, it departs Wansford for Peterborough.

The prototype that started a massive transformation to Britain's railways. Prototype Class 41 HST No. 41001 visited the Nene Valley Railway in 2016 and attracted a wide amount of people who wished to travel behind a piece of valuable history. This HST power car has been fitted with an original Valenta engine and is maintained and cared for by the 125 Group at the Great Central Railway (Nottingham) at Ruddington.

Finally, all of these images were taken between 2016 and 2018 as new stock and operators were coming into place. All images are my own and were taken within the safety rules and regulations of the railways. Remember, the railways are a dangerous place and can kill if mistreated.

The HSTs that have been working on the East Coast Main Line since the 1970s are still going strong to this day. Here, No. 43307 (No. 43107) sits at London King's Cross with the once-a-day service for Inverness. This service is known as the Highland Chieftain.

One of two specially liveried Class 91s sits at London King's Cross, awaiting departure for Edinburgh. No. 91111 was unveiled at Newcastle in 2014 in this special livery and is named *For the Fallen*, commemorating the people who had fought and fallen in the First World War. The purple stripe across the middle has facts written across it and the entire body is covered with images relating to the First World War, including the iconic poppy.

The view at the end of Platform 1 at London King's Cross allows enthusiasts to see the other trains from Platforms 2 to 8. Three Class 91s line up at London King's Cross, awaiting departure. No. 91132 (*left*) is unique for the branding that it wears, which advertises the end of mental health discrimination in the workplace, while No. 91110 (*middle*) proudly wears a Battle of Britain memorial livery.

Should a Class 91 set fail on the East Coast Main Line, they can be rescued by a DB Class 67 diesel locomotive such as No. 67004, which is seen here at London King's Cross. The sole reason they are chosen is because they can reach 125 mph, meaning that any delay is reduced.

Class 180 Adelantes operated by First Hull Trains start their journey here. No. 180111 waits to depart for Hull.

On 26 August 2017, London Euston station was closed, therefore diverting the Caledonian Sleeper from Scotland over to London King's Cross. In 2015 Serco became the new operator and started operating with different locomotives. GBRF Class 92 electric locomotive No. 92032 sits at London King's Cross, waiting time to depart with empty coaching stock (ECS) to Wembley depot, where the carriages are stored during the day.

Platforms 9 to 11 are reserved solely for the Great Northern services from East Anglia. These can be served by one of three electric multiple units (EMUs), one of which is Class 387 Electrostar No. 387102, seen waiting to leave with a service for King's Lynn.

Great Northern Class 365 Networker No. 365524 sits at London King's Cross after arriving from Cambridge. This unit will sit here for half an hour before departing again for Cambridge.

Great Northern Class 313 EMU No. 313059 arrives at Finsbury Park with a service for Moorgate. Despite there being a platform on either side of this unit, the doors will only open on the right-hand side.

After leaving the capital, the first stop is reached within 2 miles; here, Great Northern Class 365 Networker No. 365511 arrives at Finsbury Park with a service for Ely. This is a semi-fast service, stopping at seven stations before arriving at Ely under two hours later. The grey building dominating the skyline behind No. 365511 is Emirates Stadium, the ground of Arsenal football club. Many supporters alight here for the stadium and there is also a merchandise shop when leaving the station.

No book on the East Coast Main Line would be complete without an appearance from the world-famous *Flying Scotsman*. This A3 Pacific, designed by Sir Nigel Gresley and built in 1923, reached 100 mph, which was a first for a train in the UK in 1934. It has been to both America and Australia, but in this image it is only going as far as Ealing Broadway with a railtour it had brought from Scarborough.

Thameslink Class 700 Desiro No. 700036 arrives at Finsbury Park with a late-running service for London King's Cross. This service unusually started at Hitchin today, rather than Peterborough, where these services usually start.

Approaching Finsbury Park and slowing for the descent into London King's Cross is LNER Class 82 DVT No. 82220 with a service from Newcastle. It will need to go through Copenhagen and Gasworks tunnels before arriving at the London terminus.

When EMUs are taken out of service they usually run empty coaching stock (ECS) back to Hornsey depot. To avoid getting in the way of services heading out of London, they pass through on a goods line that avoids going through the station. Here, Great Northern Class 387 Electrostar No. 387111 takes this line as it heads towards Hornsey after finishing a Cambridge–London King's Cross service.

On 18 August 2018, a railtour ran from Doncaster to Eastbourne. The traction provided for this railtour was a pair of Class 47 diesel locomotives, with No. 47746 on the front and No. 47854 on the rear. It can be seen here pulling into Finsbury Park before heading off to its next stop at Kensington Olympia via the North London Line.

Sporting the remains of a bird it hit somewhere on its Down journey, Grand Central Class 180 Adelante No. 180107 passes through Finsbury Park with a service from Bradford Interchange. These services run non-stop from Doncaster to London, which can be achieved in roughly 90 minutes.

3 miles from London King's Cross is the station of Harringay, which is favoured by train enthusiasts, mainly due to the curve preceding the station. Here, LNER Class 43 HST No. 43309 in immaculate condition approaches Harringay with a service for London King's Cross.

With a friendly wave from the driver and a tone from the horn, Great Northern Class 365 Networker No. 365532 passes Harringay with a service for London King's Cross.

As it approaches journey's end with a service that started from Peterborough, Great Northern's Class 387 Electrostar No. 387106 powers through the station, heading towards Finsbury Park on a London-bound service.

Despite all the trains that pass through Harringay, it is served by a half hourly service to Moorgate which is operated using Class 313 EMUs. They always work as a pair on these diagrams as seen here as No. 313035 leads No. 313026 with one of the services for Moorgate.

There is another corner from the London-bound direction as well, which is another reason why this station is favoured by train enthusiasts. Grand Central Class 180 Adelante No. 180107 leans into it with a service for Bradford Interchange.

There are three destinations heading away from Harringay, all using the same Class 313 units. Passengers can travel on a half-hourly service to Welwyn Garden City, as Great Northern Class No. 313123 is seen forming; otherwise there is an hourly service to Watton-at-Stone on the Hertford loop line or to Stevenage, stopping at stations via the loop line.

Another East Midlands Trains Class 43 HST to grace the East Coast Main Line is No. 43061 as it leads a service bound for Leeds.

The slower services will pass through the platforms at Harringay despite not being booked to stop there. Here, Thameslink Class 700 Desiro No. 700051 heads through the station with a slow service for Cambridge.

Above and below: 1 mile further away is Hornsey and next to the station is Hornsey Traincare depot, which is the primary depot for Great Northern. During the 1970s it was extensively rebuilt in preparation for the East Coast Main Line electrification and in 2016 it was extended to allow the then new Class 700 Desiros to be maintained there too. Great Northern maintains Classes 313, 365, 387 and 700 at this depot, and because of its close proximity to London units can be dispatched to the capital quickly.

How does a unit get into Hornsey depot on the other side of the station without disrupting the services operating on the East Coast Main Line? As Great Northern Class 387 Electrostar No. 387105 pulls into the reversing sidings, the driver will then walk to the end other end of the train and will then begin to proceed over a flyover. Once the driver has gone over the flyover, they will pull into another siding outside Harringay before changing ends again and then pulling into Hornsey depot. This complex operation has to be done for every unit that needs to get into Hornsey.

On the other side of the station, a slow avoiding line can be seen. This line can be used for LNER trains coming out of Bounds Green depot. Seen outside Alexandra Palace station, LNER Class 91 No. 91117 slowly pushes its train through Hornsey, bound for London King's Cross.

Great Northern Class 365 Networker No. 365506 speeds through the station with a service for Ely.

Shortly behind the Networker was Great Northern Class 387 Electrostar No. 387102 with a service for King's Lynn. Unlike the preceding service, which will stop at Stevenage, Hitchin, Letchworth, Baldock and Royston, this service to King's Lynn runs non-stop to Cambridge.

First Hull Trains Class 180 Adelante No. 180110 passes through Hornsey with a service for Hull.

Heading towards London is Thameslink Class 700 Desiro No. 700033 with a service from Peterborough. As a result of these units arriving on the East Coast Main Line, they have replaced many of the Class 365 Networker EMUs that were the mainstay of London–Peterborough services for many years.

Great Northern Class 313 EMU No. 313052 arrives at Hornsey with a service for Watton-at-Stone. These units are still going strong on these services, despite being built over forty years ago, and with newer units having been built.

The same distance away as Hornsey lies Alexandra Palace station. Again, this is another station that is favoured by the train enthusiast community because of the track layout through the station. As First Hull Trains Class 180 Adelante No. 180109 powers away from the station, LNER Class 91 No. 91120 heads north with a service for Edinburgh Waverley.

Grand Central Class 180 Adelante No. 180108 heads through Alexandra Palace with a service for Sunderland. Named *William Shakespeare*, this Adelante previously belonged to First Great Western before being transferred to Grand Central to work alongside its existing fleet of five Class 180s.

Great Northern Class 387 Electrostar No. 387122 leads a twelve-carriage train through Alexandra Palace with a service for London King's Cross.

LNER Class 91 No. 91130 passes Alexandra Palace with a service for Edinburgh Waverley. This 91 was named *Lord Mayor of Newcastle* after celebrating the 800th anniversary of King John granting the then burgesses the power to elect a mayor of Newcastle.

Grand Central Class 180 Adelante No. 180105 slowly passes through Alexandra Palace with an empty coaching stock (ECS) movement from London King's Cross to Bounds Green depot on the other side of Alexandra Palace. Much like Hornsey depot, No. 180105 must pass over a flyover and go into a reversing siding at Bowes Park. Once there, the driver changes ends and passes through the station and into the depot.

Ferrying more passengers towards the capital with the half-hourly service for Moorgate is Great Northern Class 313 EMU No. 313029.

LNER Class 43 HST No. 43315 powers through Alexandra Palace with a service for York.

6 miles away from London lies the quiet station of New Southgate. Services such as those to King's Lynn never stop here, as shown with Great Northern Class 387 Electrostar No. 387115, which is trying to hide as it passes through.

Slow services pass through the platforms at New Southgate, again despite not stopping. Thameslink Class 700 Desiro No. 700051 glides through with a London King's Cross service.

If it wasn't for the Welwyn Garden City services, this station wouldn't see any services at all. Here, Great Northern Class 313 No. 313134 arrives with one such service. Before transferring to Great Northern, No. 313134 spent its time working around the capital for London Overground before being replaced with a new Class 378 Capitalstar EMU.

2 miles further down the line is Oakleigh Park. Much like the preceding station, it never sees any services to places such as Cambridge or Peterborough. Here, Great Northern Class 387 Electrostar No. 387116 passes through Oakleigh Park with a service from King's Lynn.

LNER Class 91 No. 91103 heads through the station with a service for Edinburgh Waverley.

First Hull Trains Class 180 Adelante No. 180113 breaks the silence with a service for Hull.

Great Northern Class No. 313029 arrives with a service for Moorgate despite the destination blind stating King's Cross.

Great Northern Class 365 Networker No. 365532 leads a service to London King's Cross through Oakleigh Park. This service started from Peterborough.

Heading for Edinburgh Waverley is LNER Class 43 HST No. 43313. The first stop for this service will be York, before stopping at Darlington, Newcastle, Berwick-upon-Tweed and arriving at Edinburgh just over four hours after leaving London.

The years are starting to take their toll on Great Northern Class 313 No. 313038 as it is seen arriving at Oakleigh Park with a service for Moorgate.

LNER Class 91 No. 91121 passes through the station with a service for Leeds. These services cover the 185 miles in just over two hours, with stops at Peterborough, Grantham, Doncaster and Wakefield Westgate.

1 mile further away is New Barnet. Here, Great Northern Class 365 Networker No. 365538 passes through with a service for Peterborough.

LNER Class 91 No. 91109 shoots through New Barnet with a service for Edinburgh Waverley.

Moments afterwards, Grand Central Class 180 Adelante No. 180103 heads for London King's Cross.

Great Northern Class No. 313041 arrives with a service for Welwyn Garden City.

1 mile further up the line is Hadley Wood, which is a unique station as there is a tunnel on either side of the station, meaning passengers can't reach the station without having to go through one. Another DB Class 90 that made it onto the East Coast Main Line is No. 90018, which passes through with a service for Leeds.

The vibrant bodywork of No. 313123 shines in the afternoon sun as it arrives with a service for Welwyn Garden City.

Hadley Wood is also favoured by train enthusiasts for the straight lines and platforms, which can be seen here as LNER Class 91 No. 91131 passes through with a service for Edinburgh Waverley.

Great Northern Class 313 No. 313028 arrives at Hadley Wood after leaving the North Tunnel. This tunnel is over 200 yards long, but the South Tunnel, which the loco will enter after leaving the station, is nearly double that length.

No. 43306 disturbs the peace of this quiet station as it charges through with a service for Newark Northgate.

East Midlands Trains lends its HST power cars to Virgin/LNER to allow its own fleet to be taken out of service for maintenance, or other reasons. The East Midlands Trains power cars are easy to identify because of their striking livery of blue, orange and red, as well as the sound that they produce; whereas the Virgin/LNER power cars are fitted with MTU engines, noisier VP185 engines are fitted to East Midlands. Breaking up the sea of red from Virgin East Coast Trains services comes East Midlands Trains HST No. 43075 with a service for Leeds.

A fast non-stop service for London King's Cross from Cambridge formed of Thameslink Class 700 Desiro EMU No. 700033 sweeps rounds the bend.

Great Northern Class 313 No. 313044 arrives at Potters Bar with a service for Moorgate.

An LNER HST set led by No. 43302, which is yet to receive its new operator's logos, passes through Potters Bar en route to London King's Cross.

Virgin East Coast Trains services do not stop at Potters Bar either, with many of its HSTs and 91s passing through the station. Here, DVT No. 82220 passes through with a service for London King's Cross.

At Potters Bar, 12 miles away from London, Great Northern Class 365 Networker No. 365528 passes through the station with a service for Peterborough. Only services for Cambridge, Moorgate and London stop at this station.

The journey is starting to gather momentum for No. 91105 as it powers through Potters Bar with a service for Leeds.

Tragedy has befallen the East Coast Main Line; this plaque is dedicated to the seven people killed and several others who were injured when on 10 May 2002 a WAGN Class 365 Networker, No. 365526, working 1T60 12:45 London King's Cross-King's Lynn derailed at speed as it passed Potters Bar station, derailing and striking the station.

In memory
of the
seven people who lost their lives
and those who were injured
in the
Potters Bar tragedy
on May 10th 2002

14 miles from London sits another quiet station; this time, Brookmans Park. Here, LNER Class 91 No. 91118 passes through with a service for Edinburgh Waverley.

Thameslink Class 700 Desiro No. 700023 slowly passes through Brookmans Park with a semi-fast service for London King's Cross.

Great Northern Class 313 EMU No. 313046 arrives at Brookmans Park on a sweltering hot day. Fortunately for the passengers, all of the windows on these units open.

Not everything that passes through Brookmans Park is entitled to the fast line; some trains make do with the slow lines. Here, Class 800 IEP No. 800304, looking a little out of place in its Great Western Railways livery, slowly heads down the East Coast Main Line before turning off for the North London Line just before London King's Cross.

Two Class 365 Networkers that haven't traded the East Coast Main Line for Scotland still make up this familiar sight as No. 365528 leads a service from Peterborough towards its final destination.

Same train, new owners as an LNER HST powered by No. 43308 passes through Brookmans Park with a service for London King's Cross. When this picture was taken LNER had only been running the East Coast Main Line for two weeks. It may not be too long before a new livery appears on this line.

Like many stations between Peterborough and London King's Cross, recent years have seen white fences installed between the slow line platforms and the fast line platforms, as seen with Great Northern Class 387 Electrostar No. 387102 on a fast service for Peterborough.

15 miles from London in rural Hertfordshire sits Welham Green. Great Northern Class 365 Networker No. 365534 passes through with a service for London King's Cross. On this day this was one of few services running on the East Coast Main Line due to Great Northern's ongoing timetable issue.

GBRF Class 66 diesel locomotive No. 66771 passes through Welham Green with a light engine movement to Cricklewood depot on the Midland Main Line. Given their top speed of 75 mph, it is unusual to see a movement like this on the fast lines.

Great Northern Class 313 EMU No. 313052 arrives at Welwyn Green with a Moorgate service.

Another freight train that makes a regular appearance on the East Coast Main Line is 4E26, Dollands Moor–Scunthorpe, which is operated by DB and worked by a Class 66 diesel locomotive. No. 66050 is seen running early at Welham Green as it makes its way north.

The sweeping curve from the London direction allows for views like this as DB Class 90 No. 90036 passes through with a service for Newark North Gate.

The unique Flying Scotsman-liveried Class 91 No. 91101 makes its presence known as it appears around the corner at Welham Green. Leading a service for Leeds, the first stop after London King's Cross for No. 91101 would be Peterborough.

A passenger looks on while Great Northern Class 387 Electrostar No. 387114 leads a Peterborough service through Welham Green.

LNER Class 43 HST No. 43318 passes through Welham Green with a service for London King's Cross. A decal proudly displayed on the side of No. 43318 boasts forty years of the InterCity 125 arriving and shrinking journey times.

17 miles from London is Hatfield. This station has again been built on sweeping curves, making for interesting photography. Here, Great Northern Class 365 Networker No. 365541 leans into the curve with a service for Cambridge. Recently in storage at Northampton, since this photograph was taken the unit has moved to Crewe.

Grand Central Class 180 Adelante No. 180106 passes through Hatfield with a service for Bradford Interchange. Coming from First Great Western, this unit has yet to receive a repaint into Grand Central's house colours of black and orange.

Virgin East Coast Trains Class 91 No. 91130 passes through Hatfield with a service for London King's Cross. The eagle-eyed reader will notice that this set is the wrong way around as No. 91130 should be on the country end rather than the London end.

Great Northern Class 313 No. 313123 slows for its station stop at Hatfield.

Another Class 800 IEP on test as No. 800103 works a mile-accumulating run from Doncaster Carr depot to London King's Cross.

Both sides of the staggered platforms at Hatfield provide great vantage points of trains passing in either direction, as Great Northern Class 387 Electrostar No. 387122 demonstrates.

Virgin East Coast Trains Class 82 DVT No. 82219 heads through Hatfield with a service for London King's Cross.

Shining in the midday sun is Great Northern Class 387 Electrostar No. 387107 with a service for King's Lynn.

20 miles away from London is the Garden City of Welwyn, which is served by Cambridge and Peterborough services, and is also the origin for the services to Moorgate. The station has an unusual anomaly in that it has four platforms but only three see regular use. Great Northern Class 365 Networker No. 365514 arrives at Welwyn Garden City with a service for Peterborough.

The early morning light illuminates No. 82212 as it heads through Welwyn Garden City with a service for London King's Cross.

After traversing Digswell Viaduct and junction, Virgin East Coast Trains Class 43 HST No. 43208 charges through Welwyn Garden City with a service for London King's Cross. This HST power car carries the nameplate *Lincolnshire Echo* after the regional newspaper based in Lincoln.

A half-hourly service to Moorgate calls at all stations from Welwyn Garden City and provides a very efficient service into the capital, with passengers being able to either change at Finsbury Park and catch the Tube or stay onboard and head to Moorgate. These services are operated by Great Northern Class 313 suburban EMUs. Here, Great Northern Class 313 EMU No. 313059 sits at Welwyn Garden City, waiting time before departing for Moorgate. These services always use Platform 4 to allow them to use the flyover to access the slow line without the need for crossing the East Coast Main Line.

Virgin East Coast Trains Class 91 No. 91129 looks resplendent in the early morning sunshine as it passes through Welwyn Garden City with a service for Edinburgh.

Being a Saturdays-only diagram hasn't stopped the Dollands Moor–Scunthorpe train from running in the form of DB Class 66 diesel locomotive No. 66135, as seen here passing through Welwyn Garden City. It will slow to a stop before Digswell Viaduct, where it will be temporarily held to allow faster trains to pass over the double-track section.

New to the East Coast Main Line but settling in well, Great Northern Class 387 Electrostar No. 387118 passes through Welwyn Garden City with a fast service for London King's Cross.

On 28 August 2017 a railtour called The Easterling ran from London King's Cross via Potters Bar and Cambridge to the seaside resort of Great Yarmouth. This tour was hauled throughout by celebrity steam locomotive A1 Peppercorn No. 60163 *Tornado*. The A1 class were built in 1948/49 but all were scrapped by 1966. A group of volunteers got together to build No. 60163 and eighteen years later *Tornado* started to steam under its own power. To this day it still operates all over the UK and interests train enthusiasts both old and new.

A further 2 miles away is Welwyn North, which is another unique station as it is the only double-track station on this section of the East Coast Main Line. The line is double track between Knebworth and Welwyn Garden City, making it a bottleneck and restraining capacity. Here, Virgin East Coast Trains Class 82 DVT No. 82200 flies out of the very attractive Welwyn South Tunnel with a service for London King's Cross.

Wasting no time in heading for the capital, Thameslink Class 700 Desiro No. 700015 passes Welwyn North with a service for London King's Cross.

Virgin East Coast Trains Class 82 DVT No. 82225 passes through Welwyn North with a service for Edinburgh Waverley. This is the same set seen facing the wrong way around at Hatfield, as the DVT should be on the London end.

Great Northern Class 365 Networker No. 365539 arrives at Welwyn North with a service for Peterborough. Before the May 2018 timetable change this station used to have an hourly service for Peterborough, but this has since been removed and passengers must change at Stevenage.

One service that has remained since the May 2018 timetable is the hourly service to Cambridge, which is formed by Great Northern Class 387 Electrostar No. 387110.

Virgin East Coast Trains Class 91 No. 91114 powers through Welwyn North with a service for Edinburgh Waverley. The sides of No. 91114 are decorated with vinyls promoting Durham Cathedral.

Great Northern Class 365 Networker No. 365520 departs Welwyn North with a slow service for London King's Cross.

An interesting blast from the past is integrated into the platform here at Welwyn North, as well as at many other stations on the East Coast Main Line. This is a logo for Network SouthEast, which used to own the stations between Peterborough and London King's Cross. Using different coloured bricks, the logo has been very well created and integrated for many years to come.

25 miles from London sits Knebworth, where Virgin East Coast Trains Class 82 DVT No. 82222 is seen passing through with a service for London King's Cross.

Moments later Virgin East Coast Trains Class 43 HST No. 43274 passes through with a service for London King's Cross.

Knebworth is served by an hourly Cambridge service. Here, Thameslink Class 700 Desiro No. 700009 works such a service.

Above and below: Most of Virgin's services do not stop at Stevenage, with Class 91 No. 91114 and Class 43 HST No. 43307 powering through to their various destinations.

Freight on the East Coast Main Line can be hard to find. One diagram that can be found, however, is a unit refurbishment move from Slade Green in London to Doncaster. Seen here at Stevenage, GBRf Class 66 diesel locomotive No. 66756 moves a Southeastern Class 465 Networker for refurbishment.

At the time of writing the Class 91s are going through a refurbishment process to improve reliability, and due to this there aren't enough to cover all the diagrams. As a result, Class 90s from DB have been hired in to cover. One of them, Class 90 No. 90019, arrives at Stevenage with a service for Newark North Gate.

Despite newer EMUs being drafted onto the East Coast Main Line, one of the stalwarts were the Class 365 Networkers, and these can still be found plying their trade. Here, No. 365541 awaits departure for London King's Cross.

Virgin East Coast Trains Class 82 DVT No. 82213 arrives at Stevenage with a service for London King's Cross.

27 miles in, and another 105 before its first stop at Grantham, First Hull Trains Class 180 Adelante No. 180109 charges through Stevenage with a service for Hull.

An hourly service to Moorgate via the Hertford loop line originates from Stevenage every day and is served by Class 313 EMUs. Here, No. 313060 awaits departure for Moorgate.

31 miles from London is Hitchin, where the line to Cambridge diverges. Class 365 Networker No. 365529 arrives at Hitchin with a service for Cambridge.

Hitchin is only served by Great Northern/Thameslink, with services to/from London King's Cross, Cambridge and Peterborough. The hourly service from Cambridge to London King's Cross headed by No. 700039 arrives at Hitchin.

Another Class 90 hire-in from DB sees No. 90029 passing through Hitchin with a service for Newark North Gate.

Virgin East Coast Trains Class 43 HST No. 43272 powers through, bound for London King's Cross.

First Hull Trains Class 180 Adelante No. 180113 passes Hitchin with a service for London King's Cross.

In its striking livery of black and orange, Grand Central Class 43 HST No. 43468, a former DVT, now a power car, heads towards London King's Cross.

Virgin East Coast Trains Class 91 No. 91122 makes good time as it heads further north towards Peterborough.

Not all Great Northern/Thameslink services stop at Hitchin, with the operators providing a mix of both fast and slow services to their destinations. Seen here, Class 387 Electrostar No. 387124 *Paul McCann* provides a fast service to Ely.

37 miles from London is Arlesey and Thameslink Class 700 Desiro No. 700135 passes through the station with a service for Peterborough. The service was supposed to stop here and was announced as the next service as it passed through, unknowingly to the passengers on the platform.

LNER Class 43 HST No. 43206 passes Arlesey with a service for Leeds.

East Midlands Trains Class 43 HST No. 43061 passes Arlesey with a service for London King's Cross.

After a successful test run down to London King's Cross, No. 800103 heads back to Doncaster.

Promoting a very colourful advertisement for the 'Great Exhibition of the North' on its bodyside, No. 91106 heads towards Edinburgh Waverley.

First Hull Trains Class 180 Adelante No. 180109 heads through Arlesey with a service for London King's Cross.

Great Northern Class 365 Networker No. 365539 arrives at Arlesey with a Peterborough service. This station was originally closed in 1960 and was rebuilt by Network SouthEast, being reopened in 1988. It has since seen a substantial rise in passenger numbers.

Virgin East Coast Trains Class 43 HST No. 43274 heads through Arlesey with a service for London King's Cross. Somewhere during this journey it managed to gain an unwanted addition on the windscreen.

41 miles from London is Biggleswade station, and here LNER Class 91 No. 91129 passes through with a service for York.

Grand Central Class 180 Adelante No. 180105 passes through Biggleswade with a service for Bradford Interchange.

Another Class 90 hire-in from DB was No. 90039, seen passing through as it works a service to Newark North Gate.

LNER Class 82 DVT No. 82213 heads towards London King's Cross in the mid-afternoon sunshine.

Biggleswade is served by an hourly Peterborough service, and here Great Northern Class 387 Electrostar No. 387112 arrives with one such service.

Great Northern Class 365 Networker No. 365522 arrives at Biggleswade with a service for London King's Cross, while hot on its heels is LNER Class 82 DVT No. 82203.

Still requiring rebranding, LNER Class 43 HST No. 43319 heads through Biggleswade with a service for London King's Cross.

44 miles from London and sitting in the county of Bedfordshire is Sandy. An LNER Class 82 DVT in promotional Flying Scotsman livery heads through this quiet station with a service for London King's Cross.

Being driven by another happy driver, LNER Class 43 HST No. 43290 passes through Sandy, bound for London King's Cross.

DB Class 90 No. 90039 heads back towards Newark North Gate after a brief stop at London King's Cross.

LNER Class 91 No. 91132 is at the helm with a service for Leeds.

Another day sees No. 800103 accumulating more miles on the East Coast Main Line as it passes through Sandy on a test run to London King's Cross.

Great Northern Class 387 Electrostar No. 387111 arrives at Sandy with a service for Peterborough.

The Class 91s were built with a blunt end cab to allow them to work passenger trains in the day and then freight trains and sleeper trains at night, but this never materialised. Now they use their blunt end should there be a fault with their No. 1 cab or the DVT; or, as seen here at Sandy, light engine movements. Here, No. 91108 heads to Bounds Green depot from Doncaster.

Even rain clouds have a silver lining, and during a very heavy isolated shower at Sandy First Hull Trains Class 180 Adelante No. 180111 feels the brunt of it with a service for Hull. This weather was a much-needed and appreciated change after the crippling heatwave that had hit the country in the previous weeks.

Just over 50 miles from London and getting very close to Peterborough is St Neots in Cambridgeshire. Grand Central Class 180 Adelante DMU No. 180108 passes through with a service for Sunderland.

No Virgin/LNER services stop at St Neots, so passengers require the half-hourly service to Peterborough to get trains to the north. Here, Virgin East Coast Trains Class 43 HST No. 43320 heads through the station with a service for Leeds.

Another East Midlands Trains Class 43 HST power car on hire to Virgin East Coast Trains, No. 43075 powers through St Neots with a service for Leeds.

Despite DB Class 90 electric locomotive No. 90039 doing all the work, LNER Class 82 DVT No. 82218 leads the train for London King's Cross.

On weekdays, passengers can travel from Cambridgeshire through to Horsham in West Sussex with a direct service that runs via London, Croydon and Gatwick Airport. These services are only operated by Class 700 Desiros. Here, No. 700134 is seen arriving at St Neots with one of the half-hourly services.

Virgin East Coast Trains Class 91 No. 91103 passes St Neots with a service for Newark North Gate.

Nearing journey's end after travelling for over two hours, Thameslink Class 700 Desiro No. 700149 departs St Neots with a service for Peterborough. There will be one more stop at Huntingdon before reaching journey's end.

The last station before Peterborough is Huntingdon, 58 miles away from London. Here, Virgin East Coast Trains Class 91 No. 91128 passes through with a service for Edinburgh Waverley. Seen on the side of No. 91128 is a nameplate for *Intercity 50*, commemorating fifty years of the Intercity name. This was unveiled at London King's Cross in July 2016.

No Virgin East Coast Trains/LNER services stop at Huntingdon station, as seen here as No. 43272 powers through with a service for London King's Cross.

Great Northern/Thameslink provides a half-hourly service to London King's Cross on weekends and Horsham on weekdays. A pair of Great Northern Class 365 Networkers led by No. 365522 sit at Huntingdon with a service for London King's Cross.

Thameslink Class 700 Desiro No. 700152 arrives at Huntingdon with a service for Peterborough.

Much like Virgin/LNER, Grand Central services do not stop at Huntingdon either.

Virgin East Coast Trains Class 82 DVT No. 82225 passes through the station with a service for London King's Cross.

The sun shines brightly on the attractive colours of First Hull Trains Class 180 Adelante No. 180109 as it heads towards Hull.

Making a loud racket as it passes through Huntingdon is East Midlands Trains Class 43 HST No. 43044. With a complete rake of East Midlands Trains Mk 3 carriages, it heads for London King's Cross.

76 miles away and at least an hour's travelling from London is Peterborough. Great Northern Class 321 EMU No. 321405 rests before its long journey back to London King's Cross. Great Northern runs a mix of slow and fast services to London King's Cross, although passengers can now reach further away places such as Gatwick Airport and Horsham as Thameslink introduced these newer services from 2018. This EMU has since transferred from Great Northern, but still sees work out of London, albeit from Liverpool Street.

Peterborough is a hotspot for any freight train enthusiast as the three main freight operating companies, DB, GBRF and Freightliner, can be seen passing through. Crew changes regularly occur at Peterborough, and here DB Class 66 diesel locomotive No. 66015 is being prepared by a new driver for the journey to Mountsorrel in the East Midlands.

A fast service despite being held at a red signal. Grand Central Class 180 Adelante No. 180105 awaits a proceeding aspect in the evening sunshine as it heads north towards Bradford Interchange.

Above and below: As they need to be checked for faults and have to accumulate miles before they can be accepted into traffic, more and more Class 800 IEPs are starting to be tested on the East Coast Main Line. On two separate occasions they have been spotted at Peterborough on test. During July 2017, Great Western Railways Class 800 IEP No. 800003 sits at Peterborough on test before transferring over to the Great Western Main Line. Four months later, Virgin East Coast Trains Class 800 'Azuma' IEP No. 800101 awaits departure for Doncaster under unfriendly skies.

Peterborough has seen major investment in the past to allow for extra capacity on the East Coast Main Line. Previously this was the southbound fast line, until 2013, when a new platform was installed to allow other services to use Platforms 1 and 2 and not hold up Virgin's services. The platform is being put to good use here as No. 43367 awaits departure for London King's Cross. No. 43367 wears the nameplate *Deltic 50 1955–2005*, an ironic name as the Deltic was replaced by the HST on fast services on the East Coast Main Line.

Even though Peterborough is a major station on the East Coast Main Line, a proportion of Virgin East Coast Trains/LNER services don't stop here either, with some first stopping at Grantham, Doncaster or York after London King's Cross. Located in the middle of the station, nothing can be missed going through on the fast line. Here, Class 91 electric locomotive No. 91101 is spotted wearing a special Flying Scotsman livery. This is the second rendition of the livery, as it was changed by Virgin. The loco previously wore East Coast's original purple livery, but was given this livery after East Coast introduced the 05.40 service from Edinburgh to London King's Cross, which stops only at Newcastle.

From time to time power cars may need to be hired in to keep services running. During April 2016, Virgin East Coast Trains hired in Arriva CrossCountry power car No. 43321 for a short period. It is seen arriving at Peterborough with a service for London King's Cross.